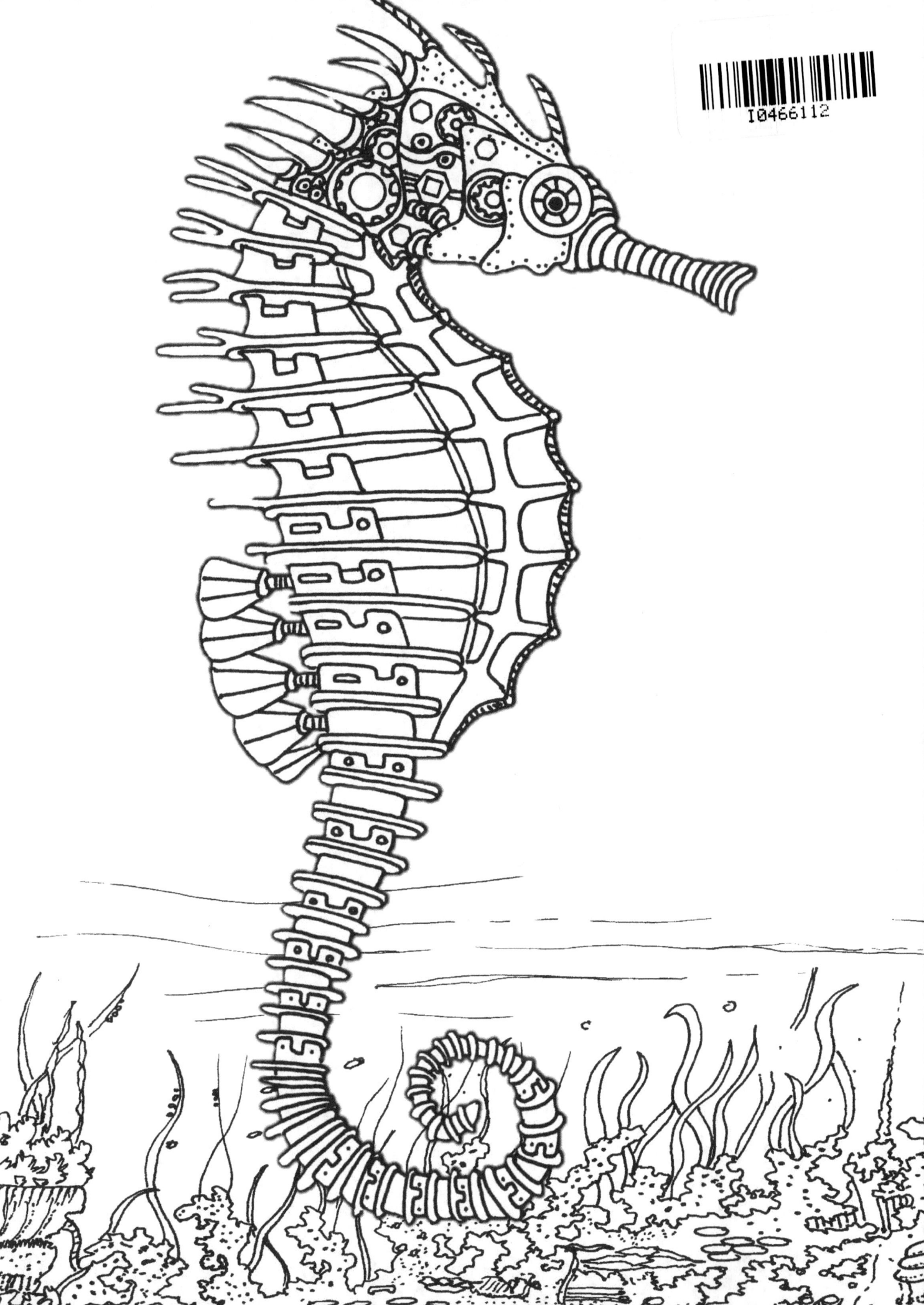

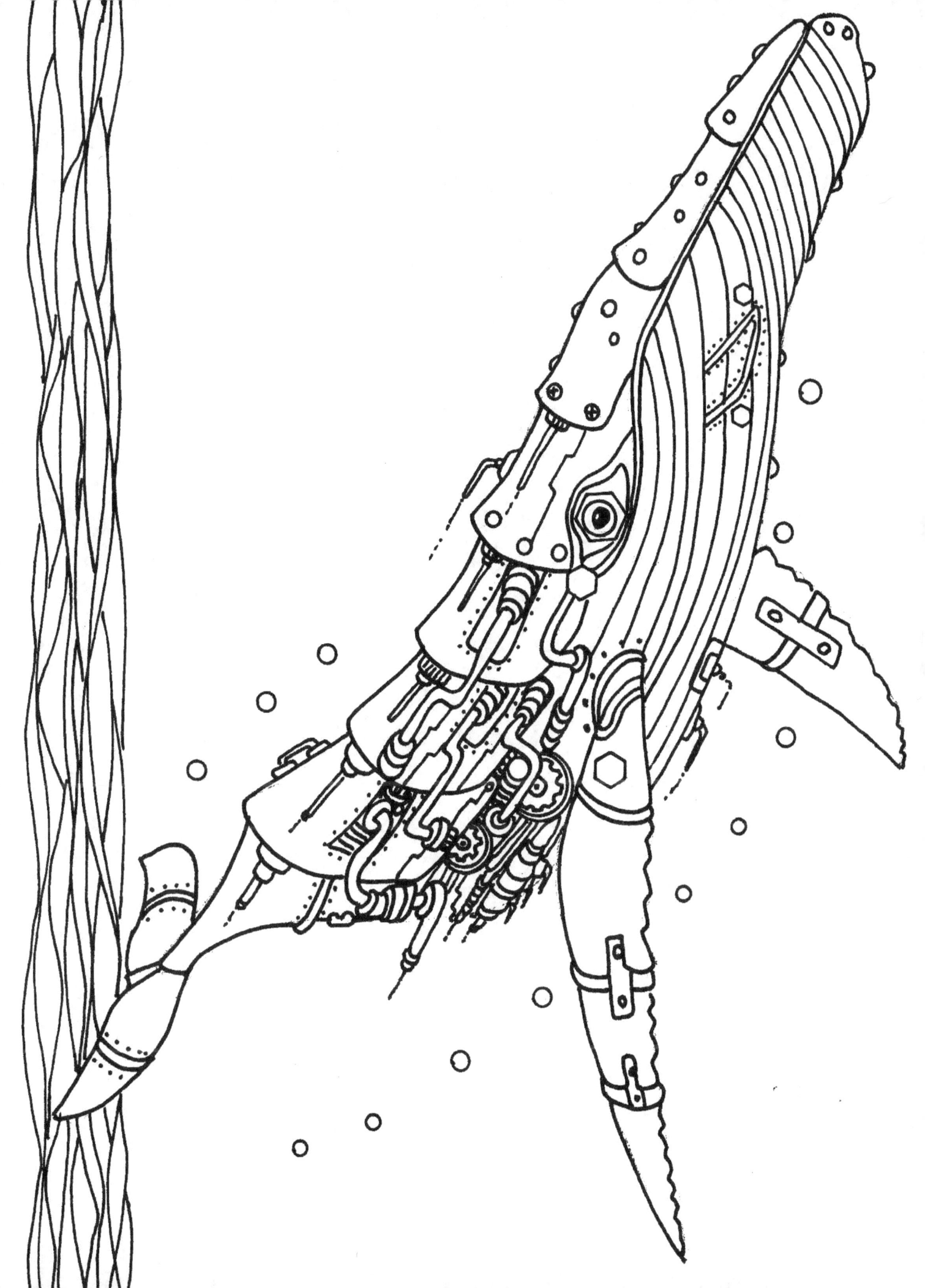

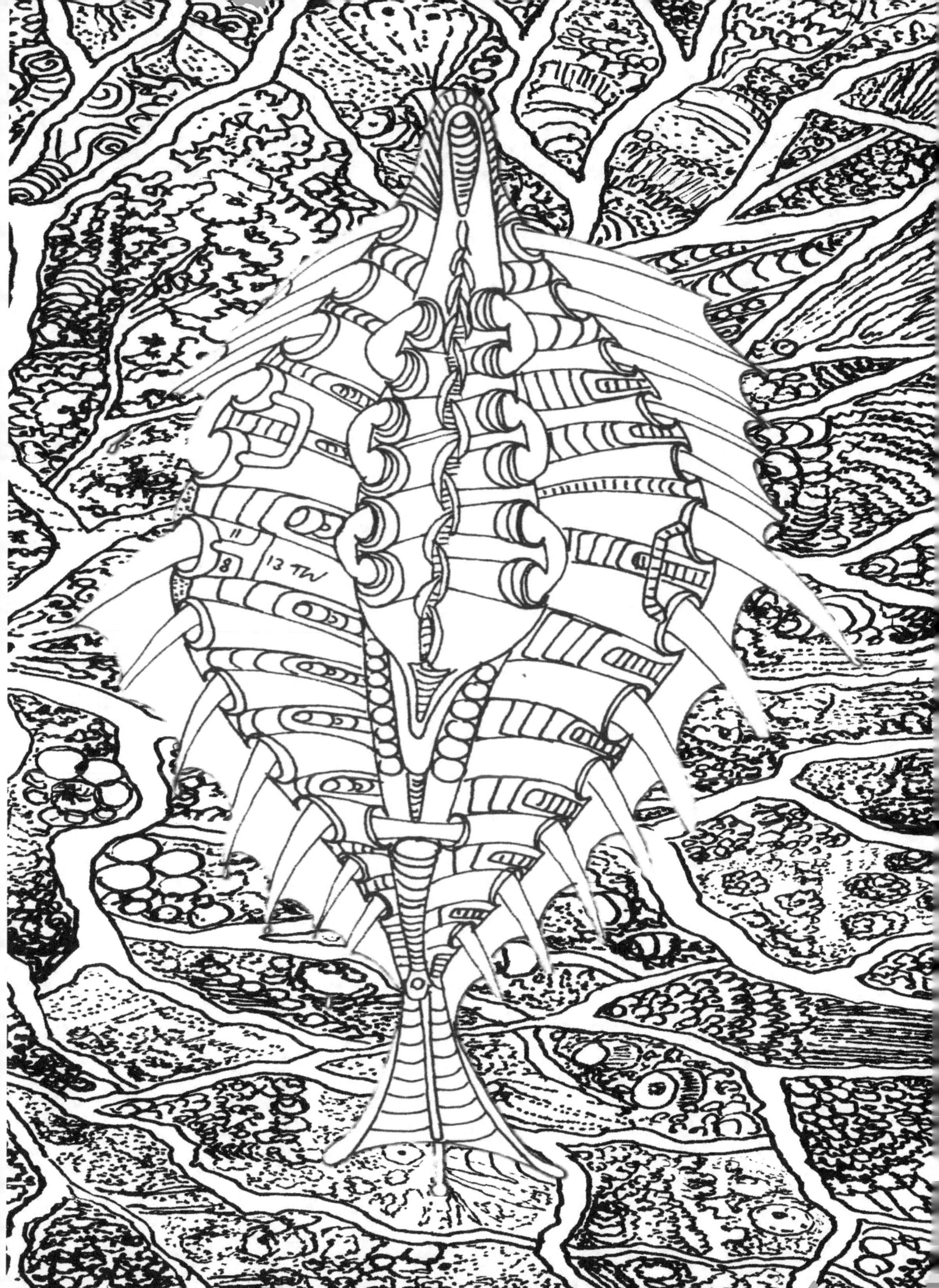

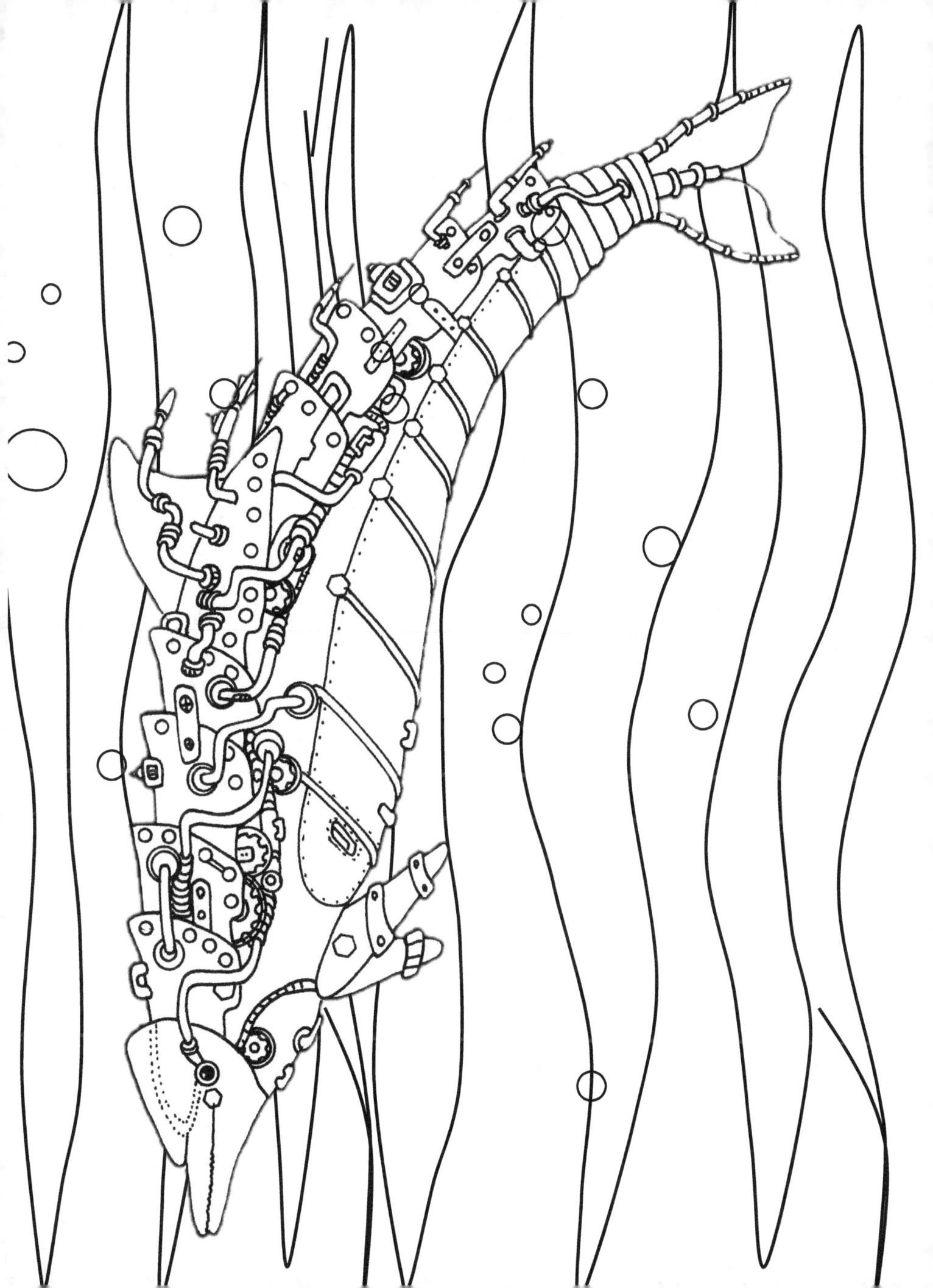

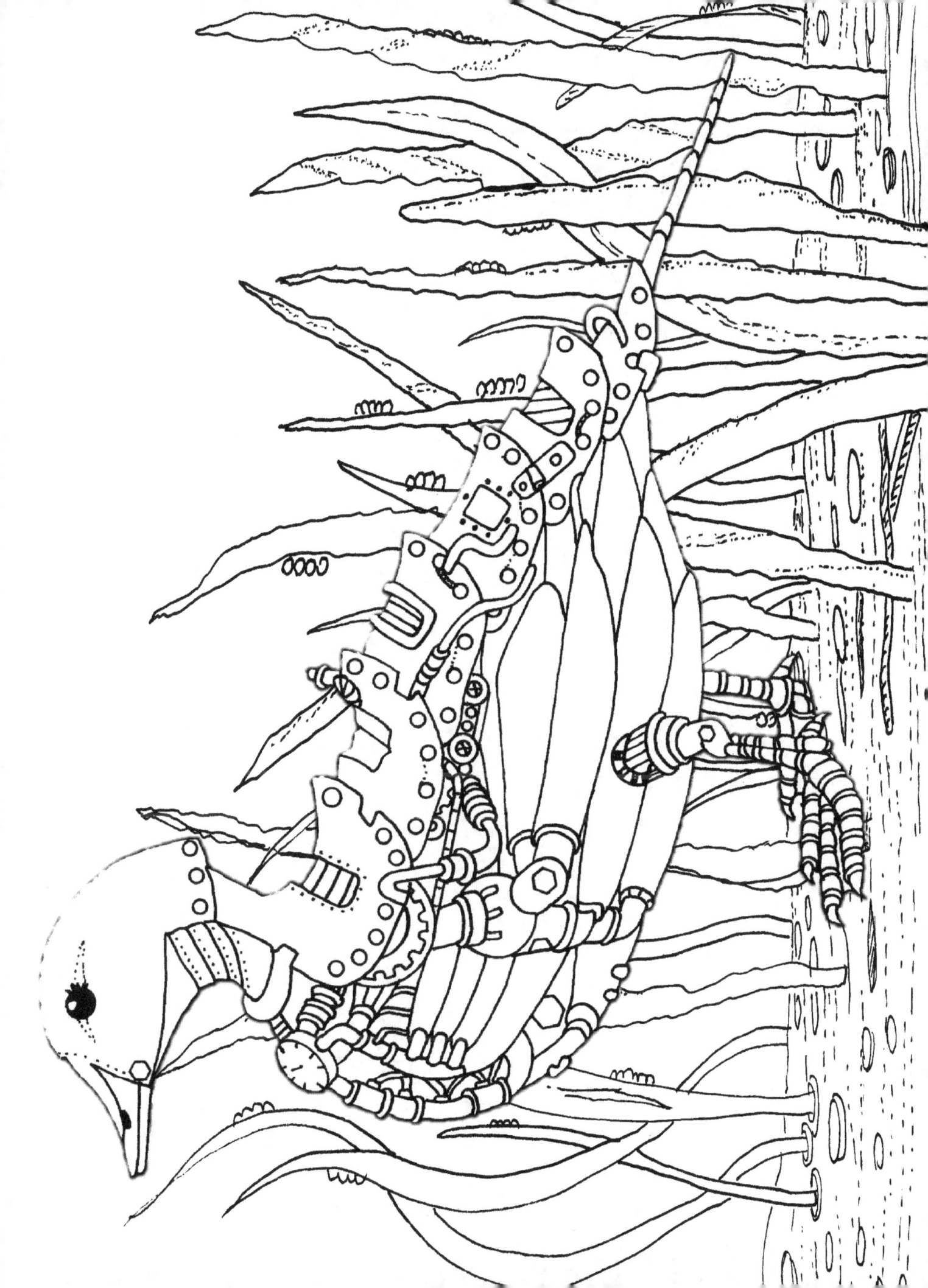

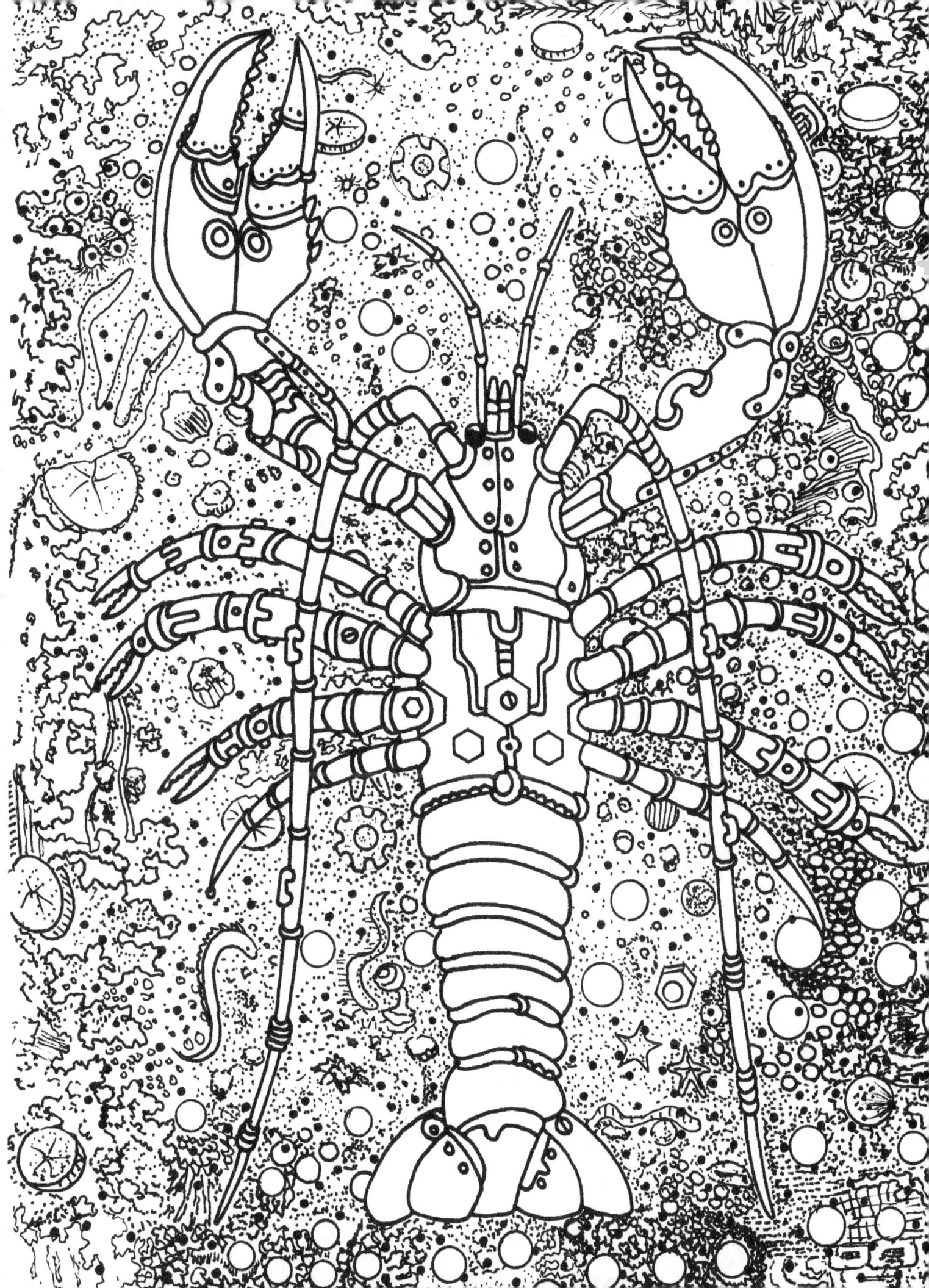

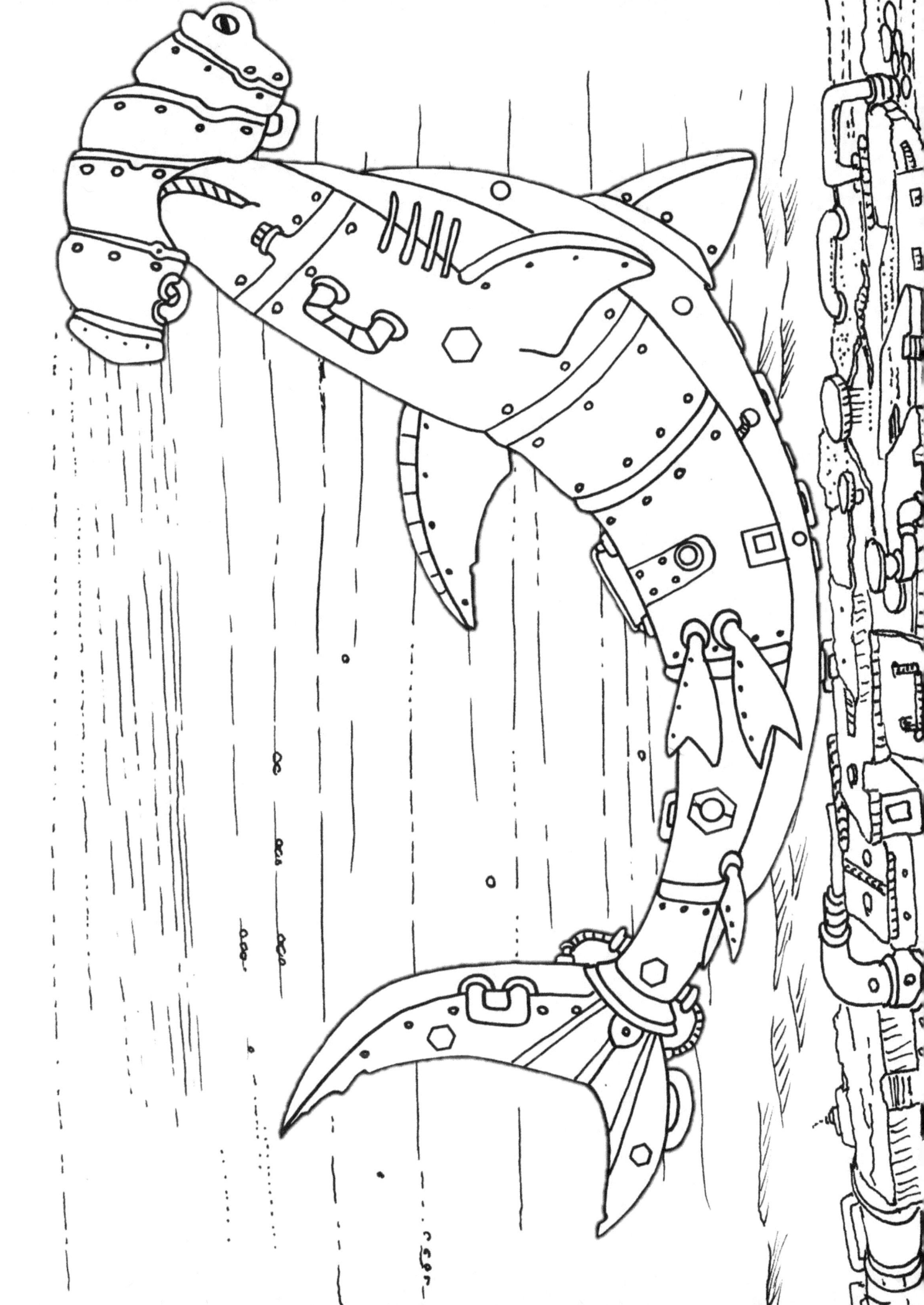

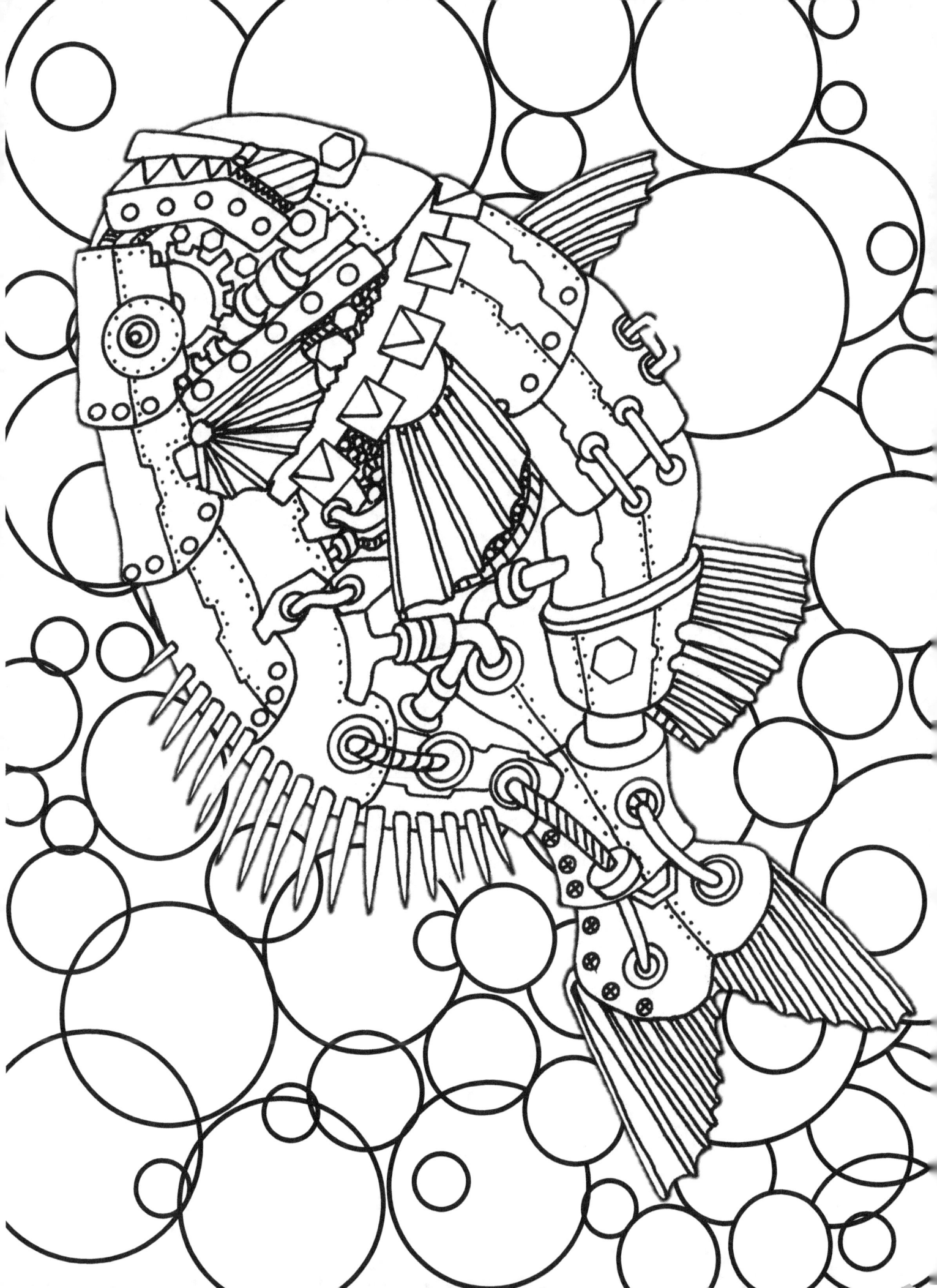

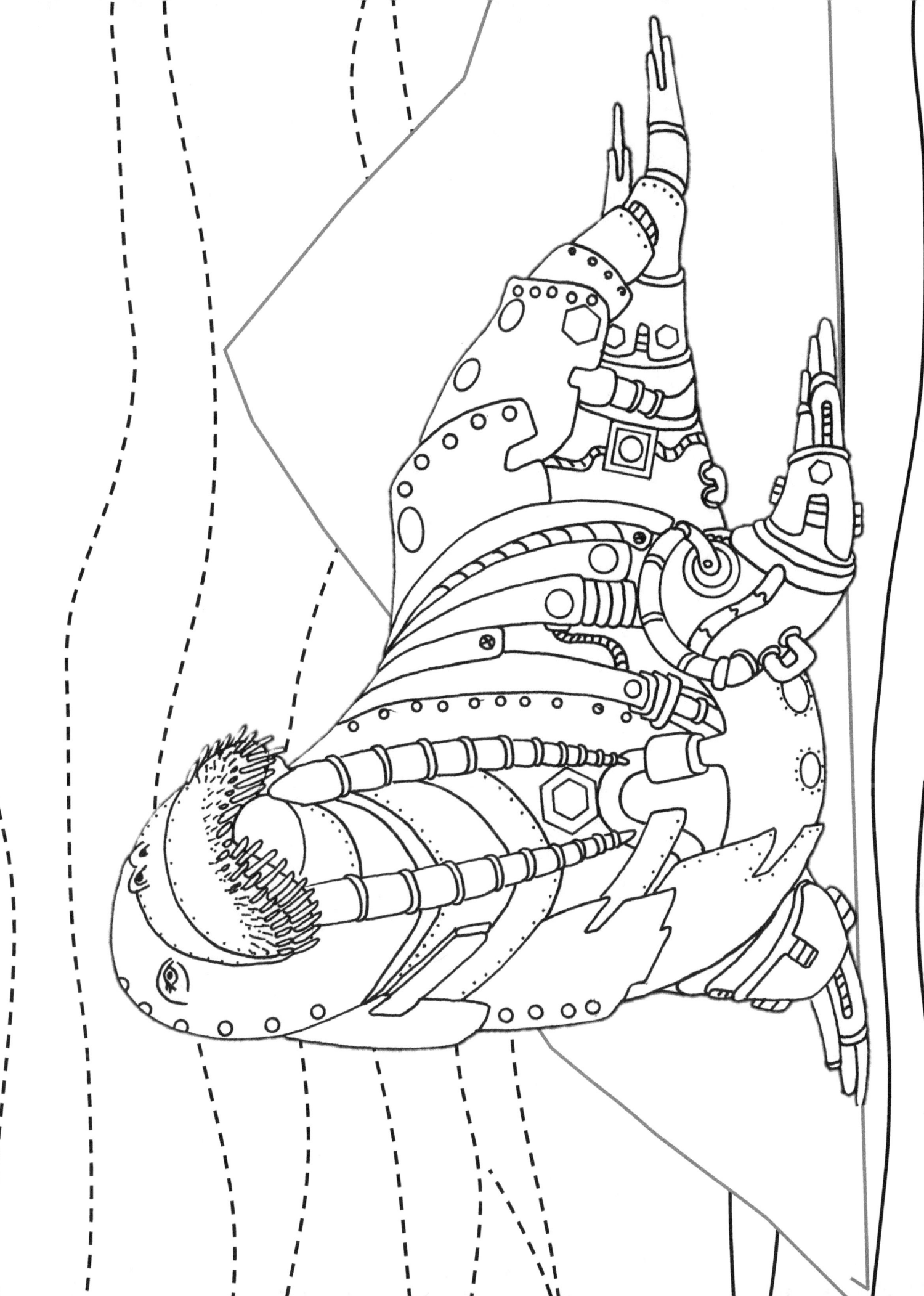

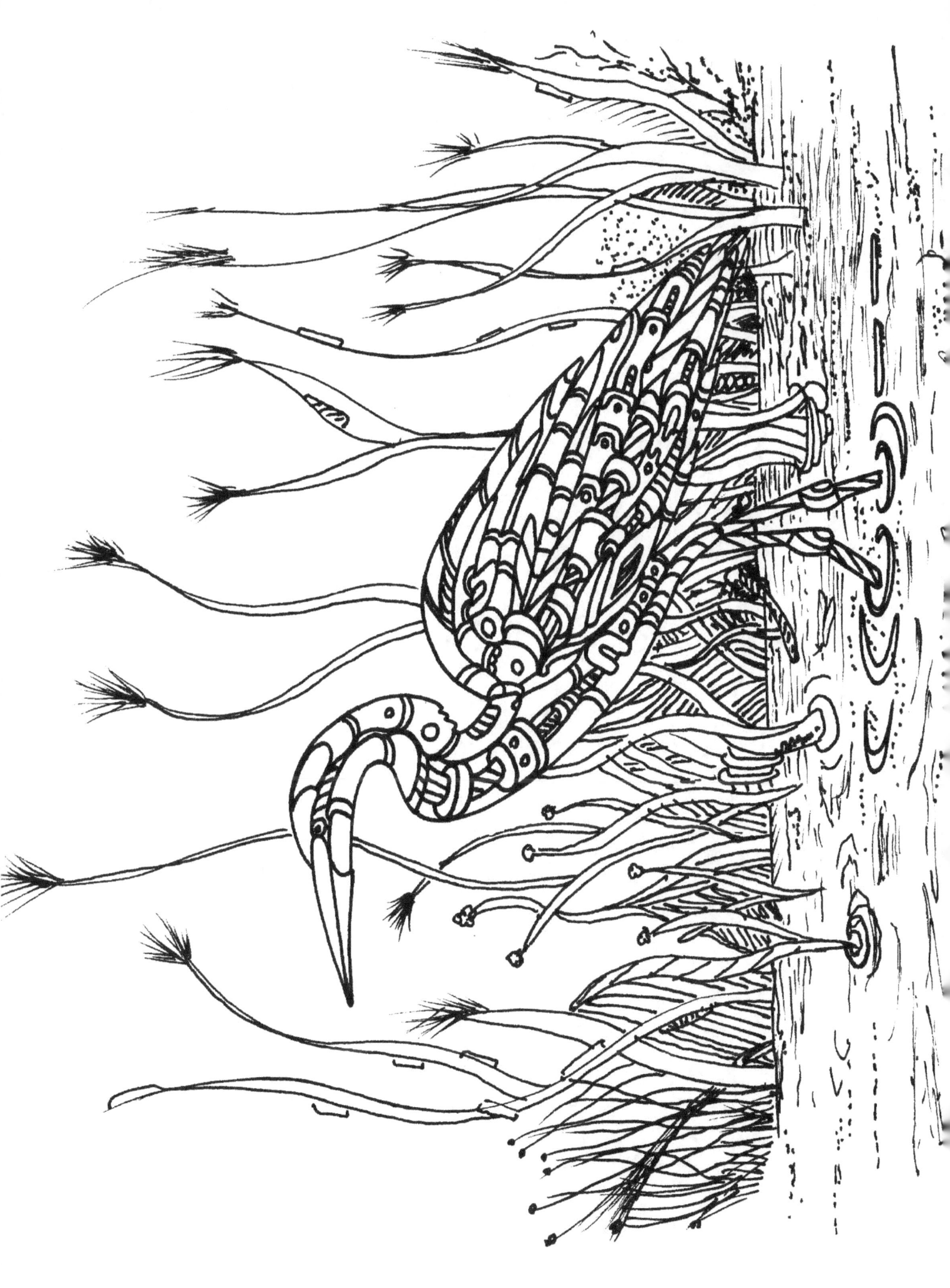

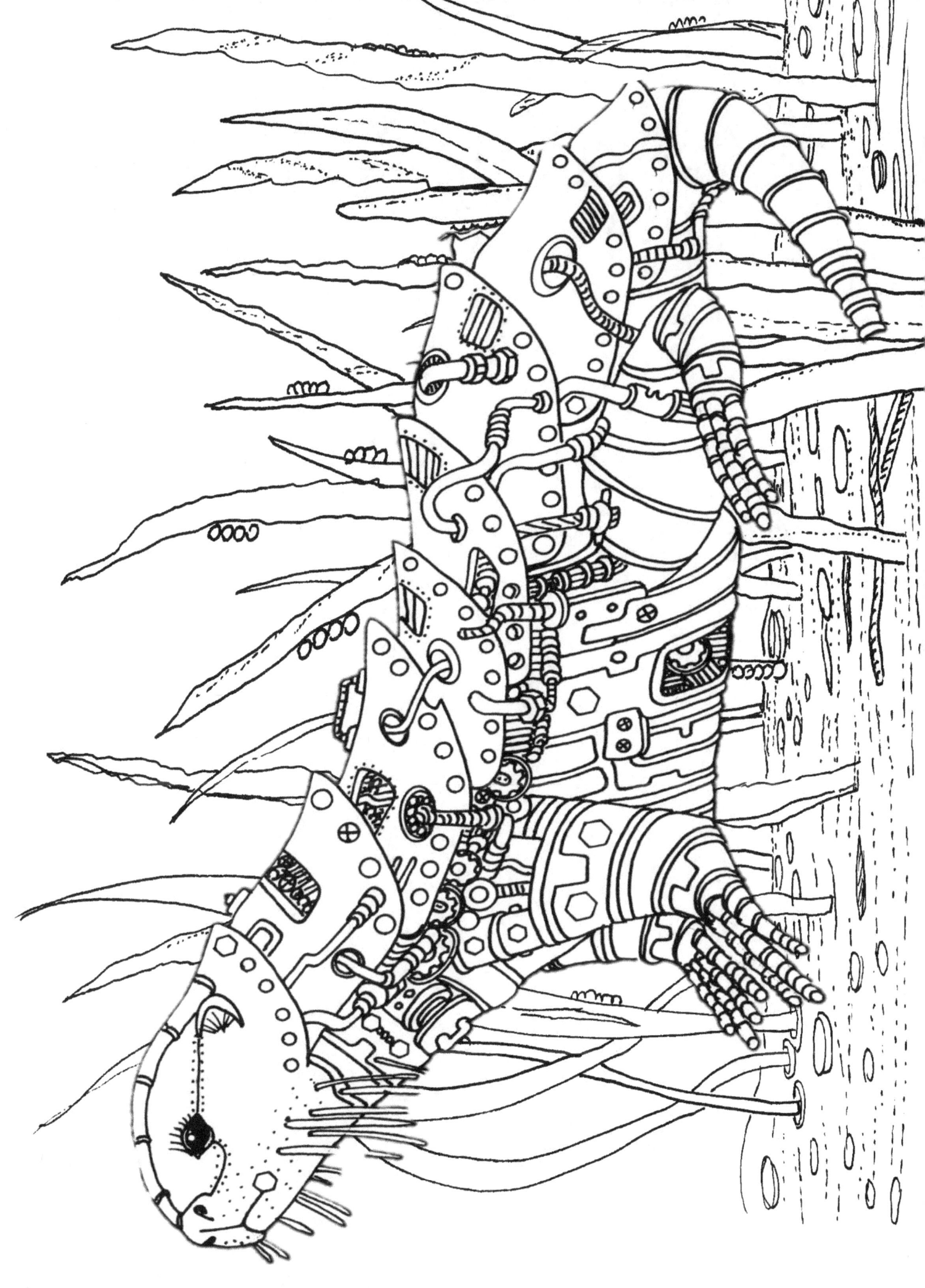

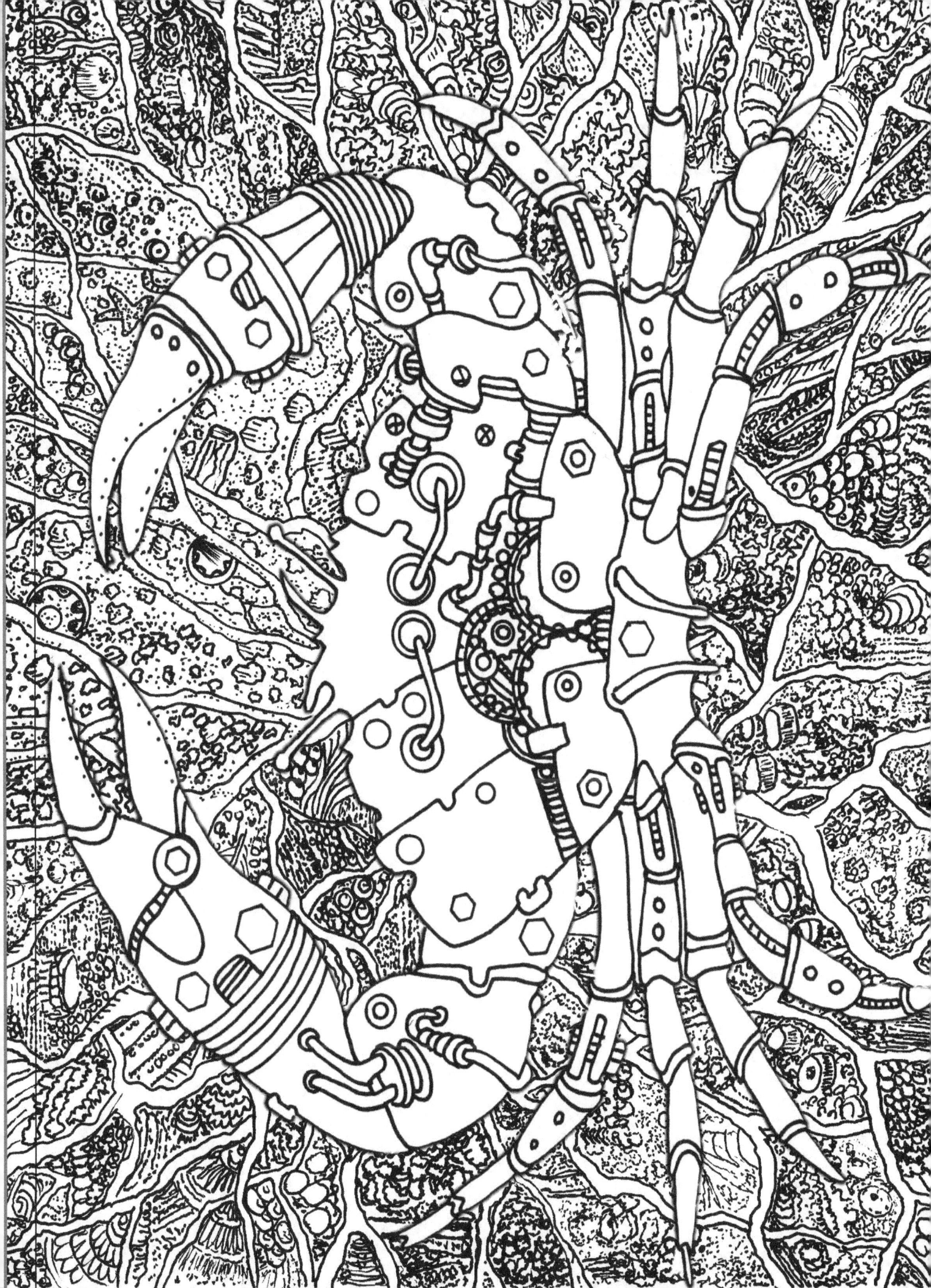

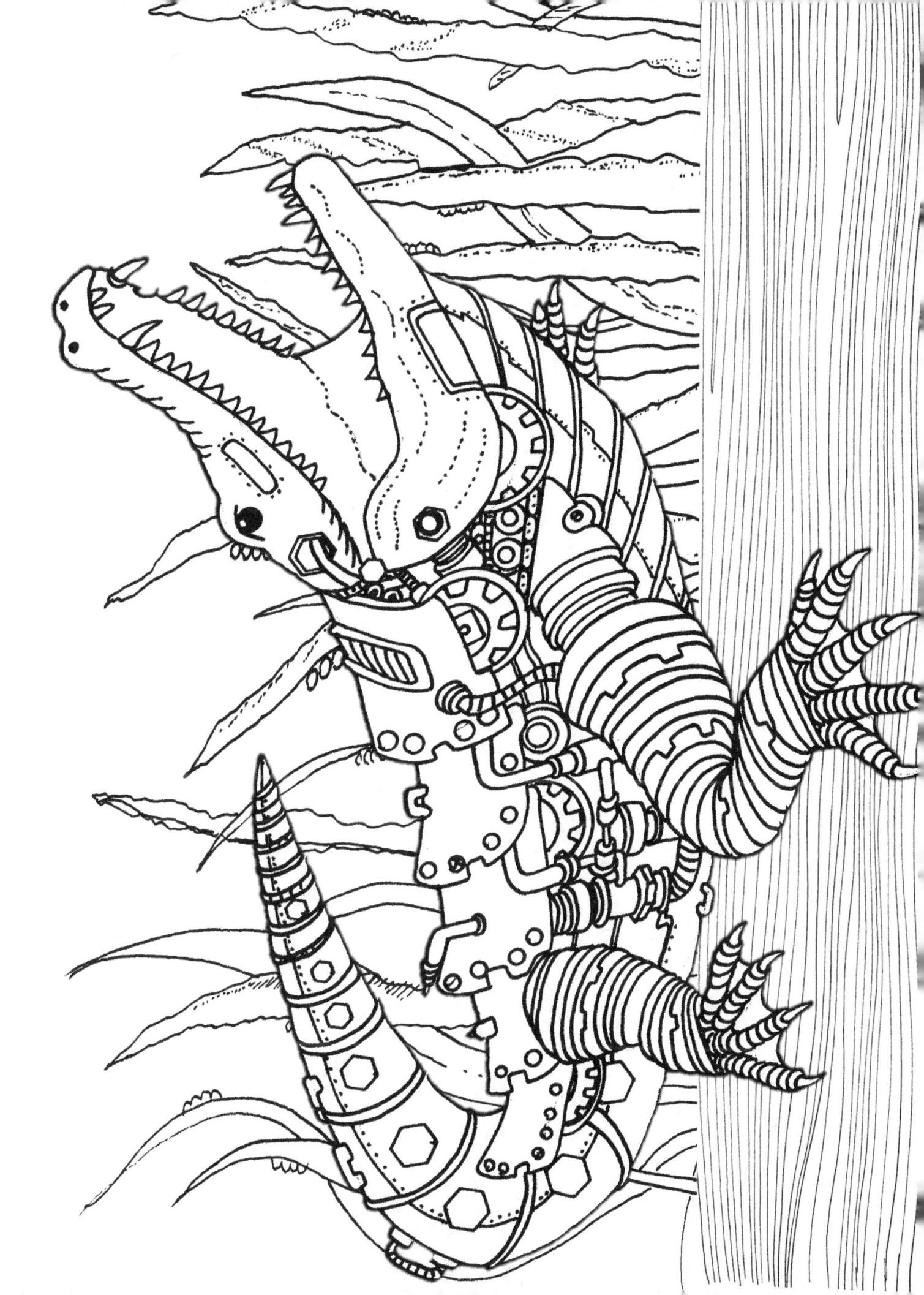

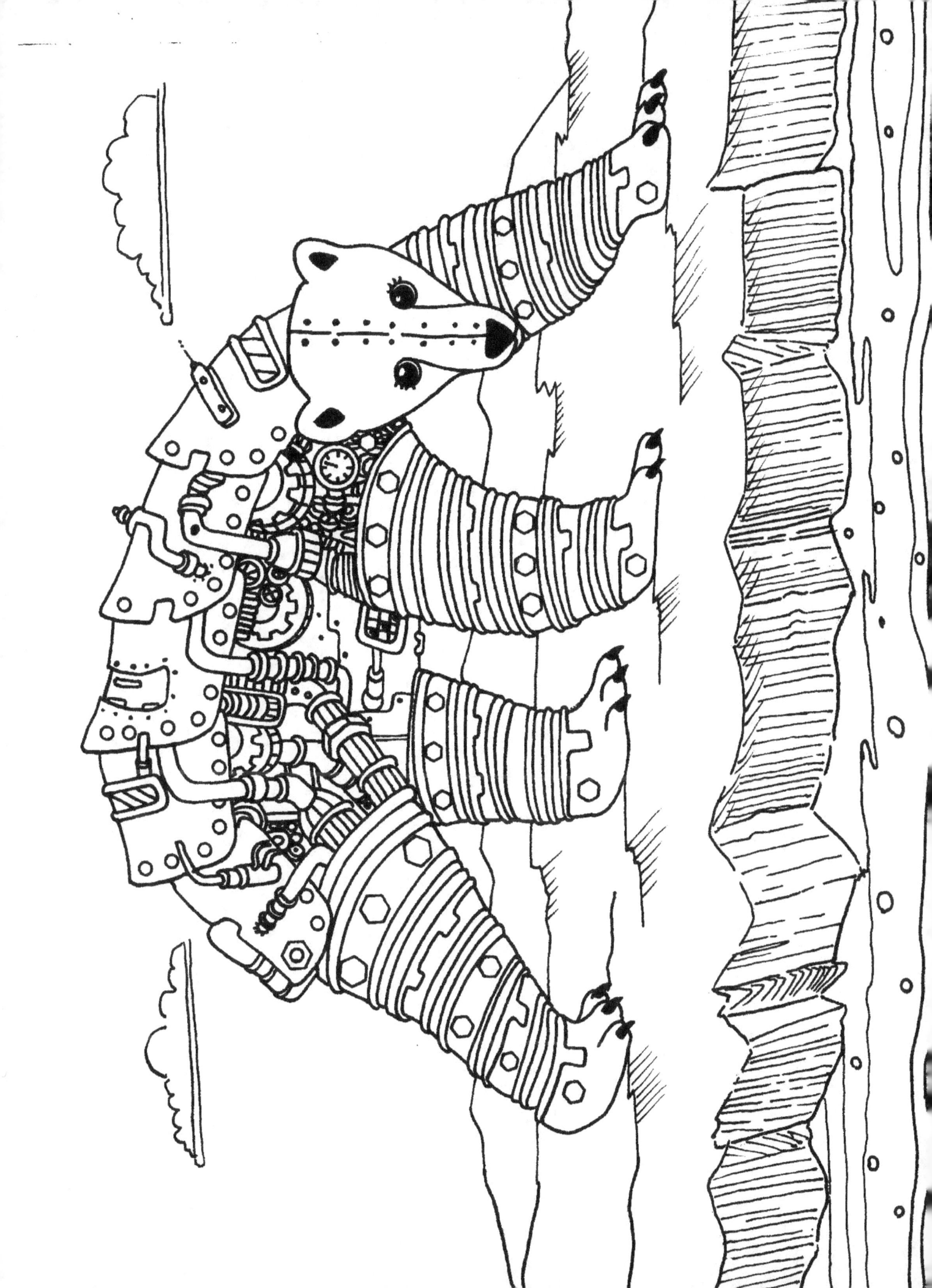

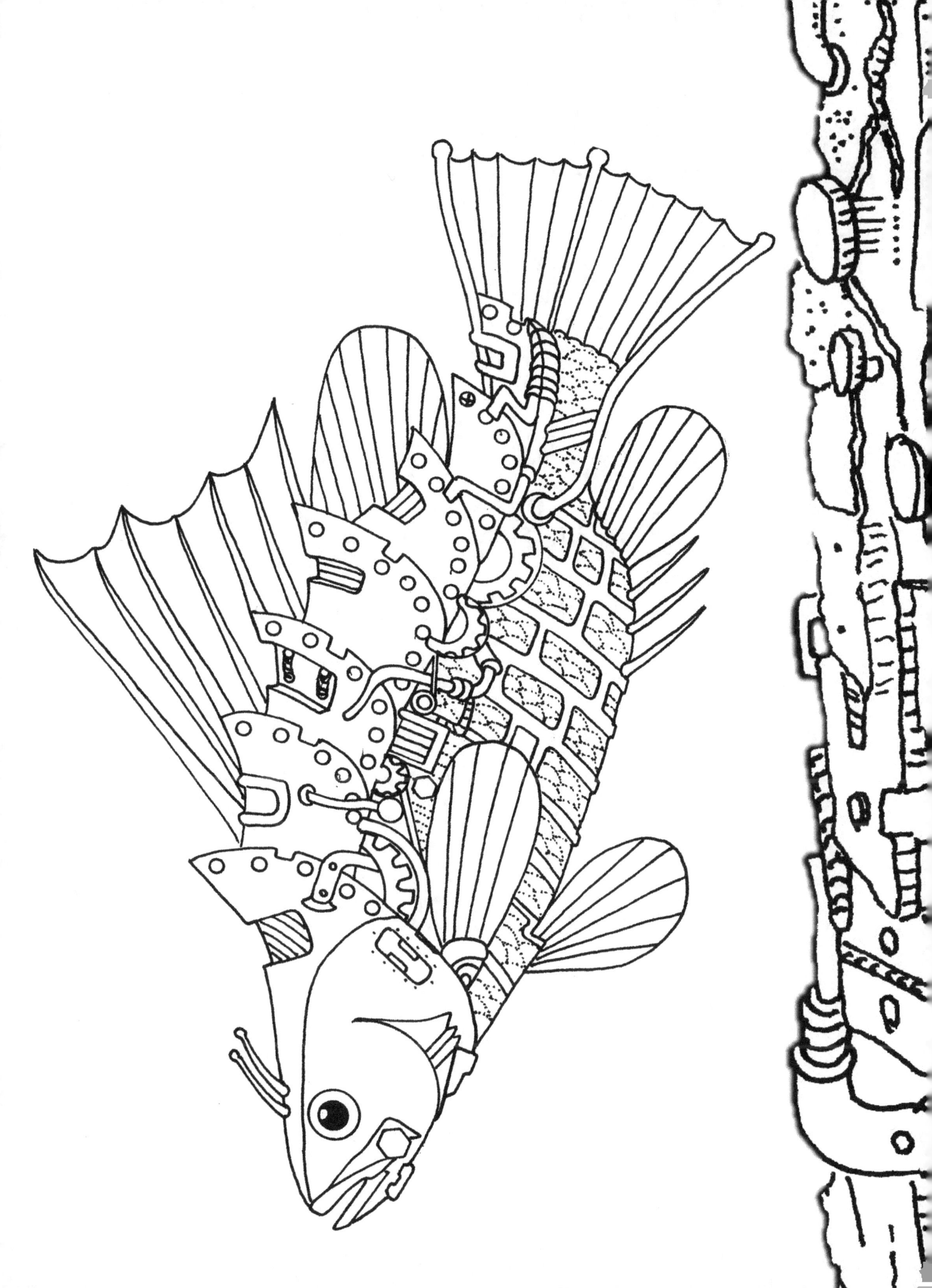

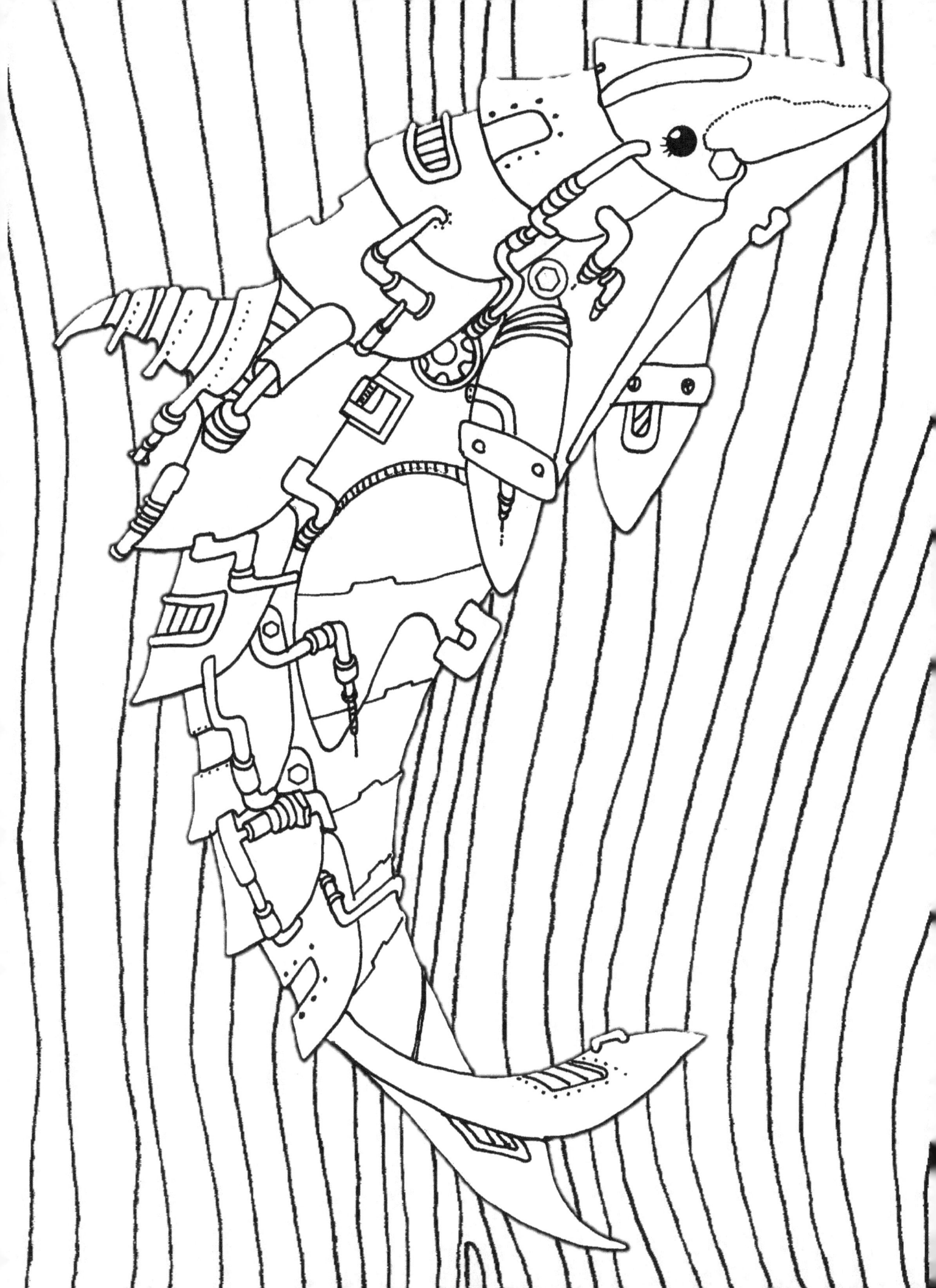

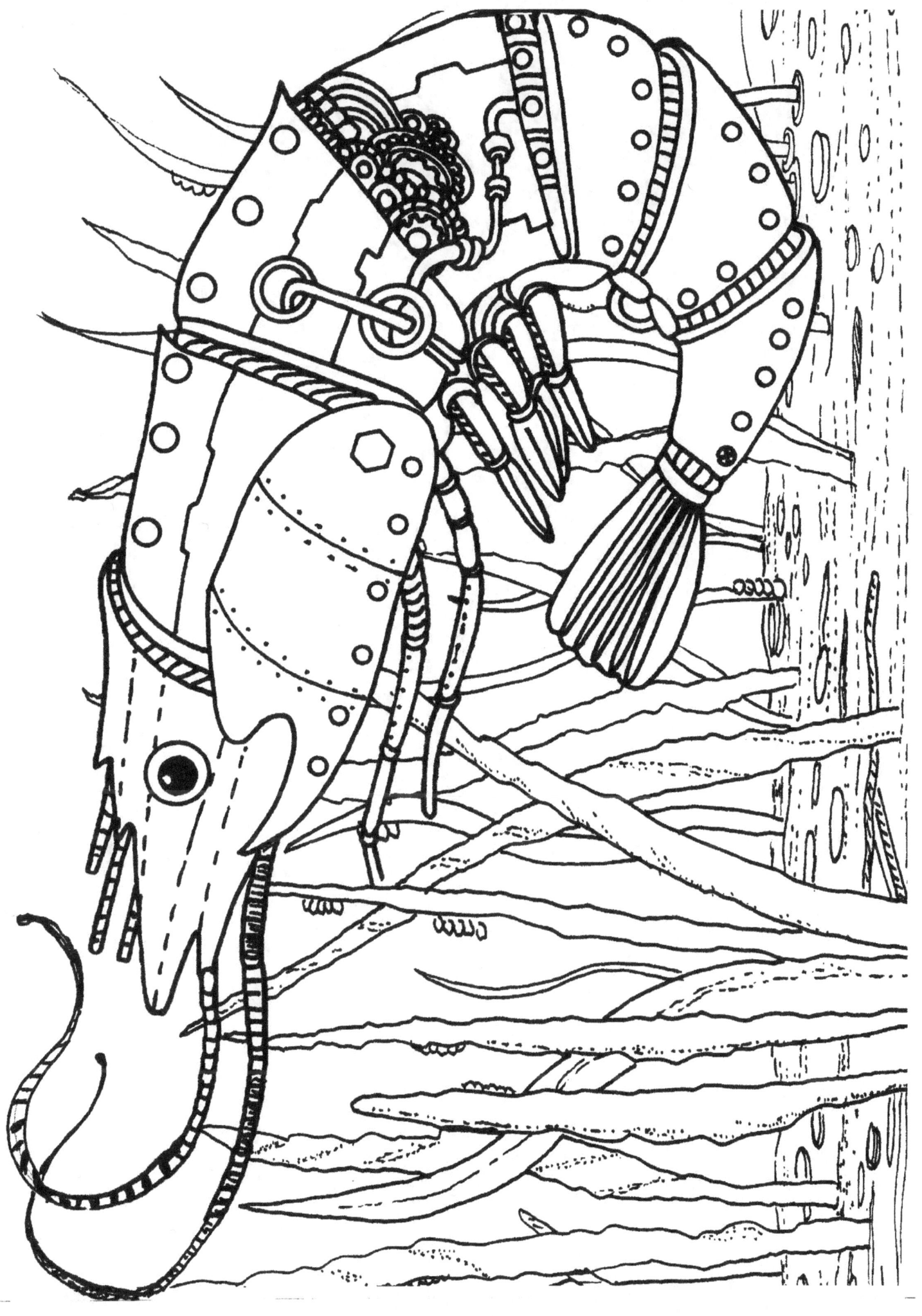

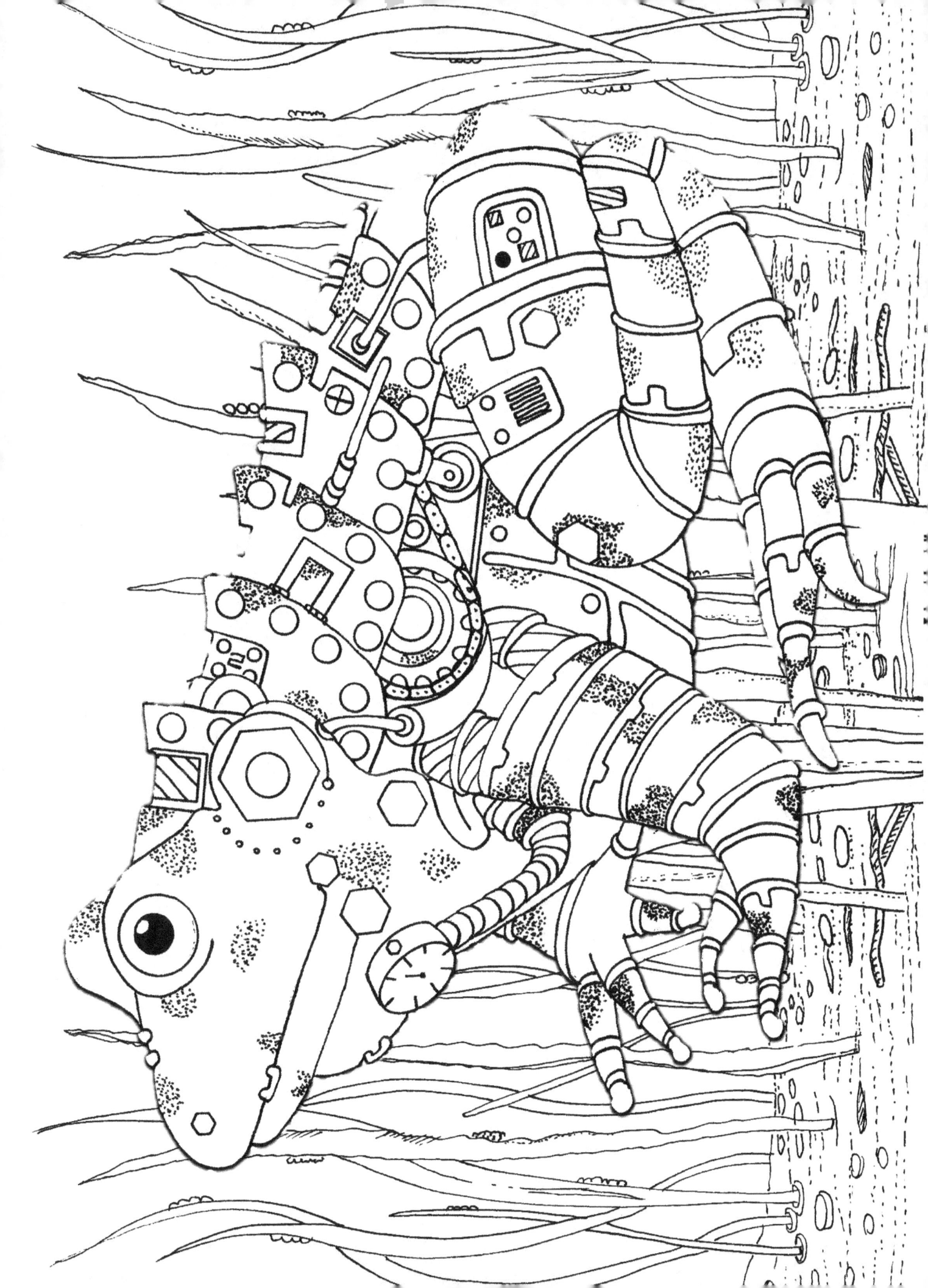

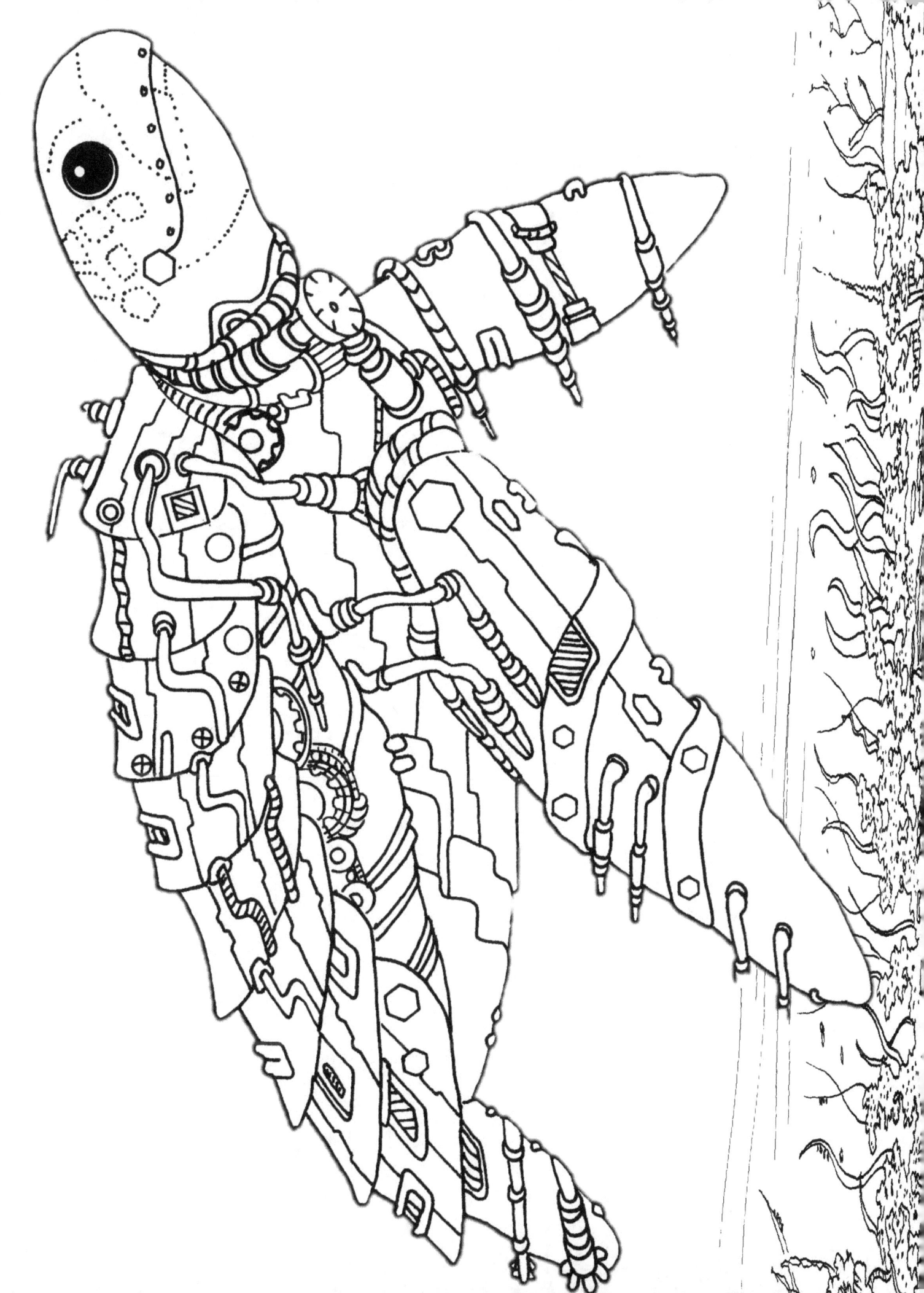

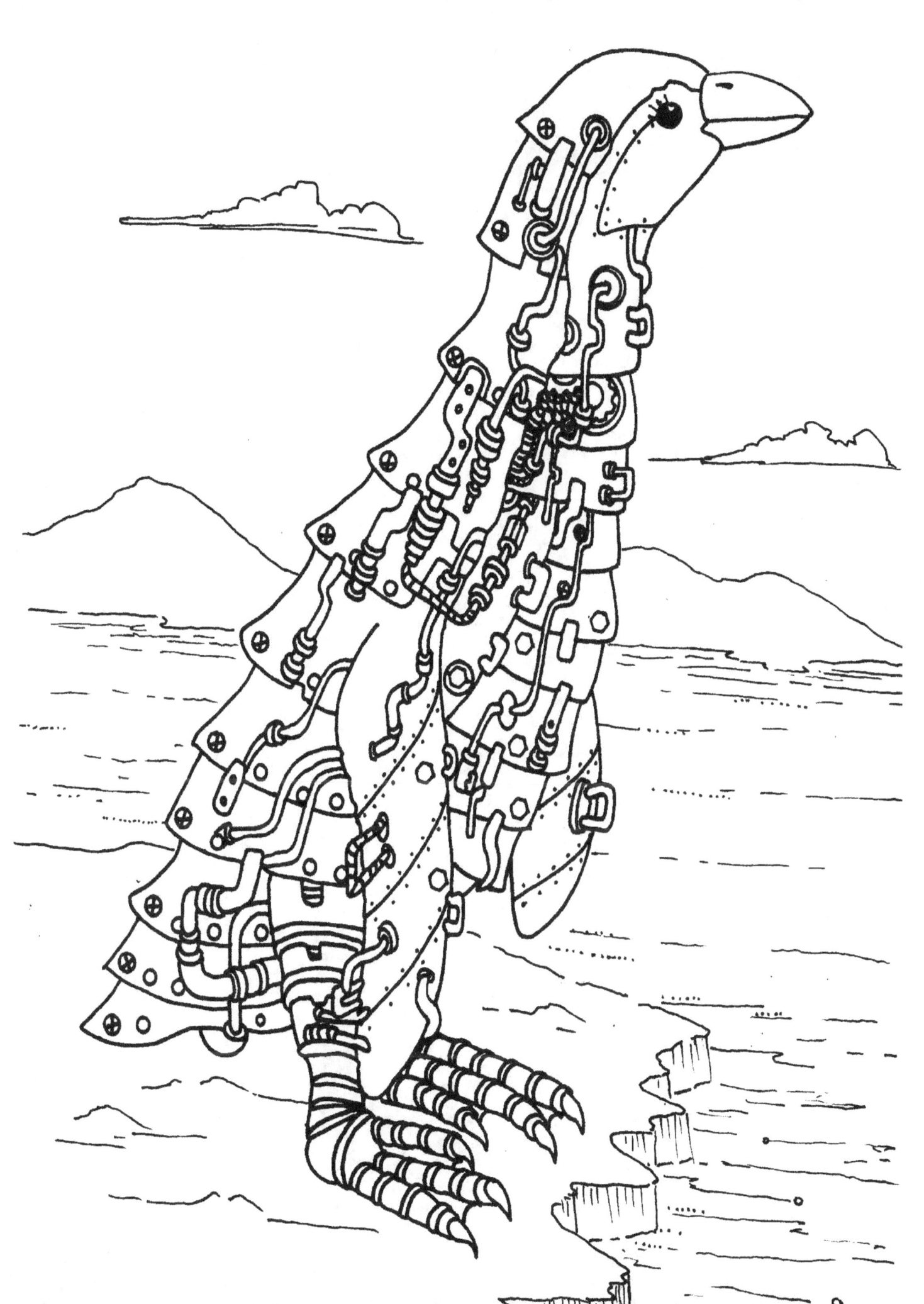

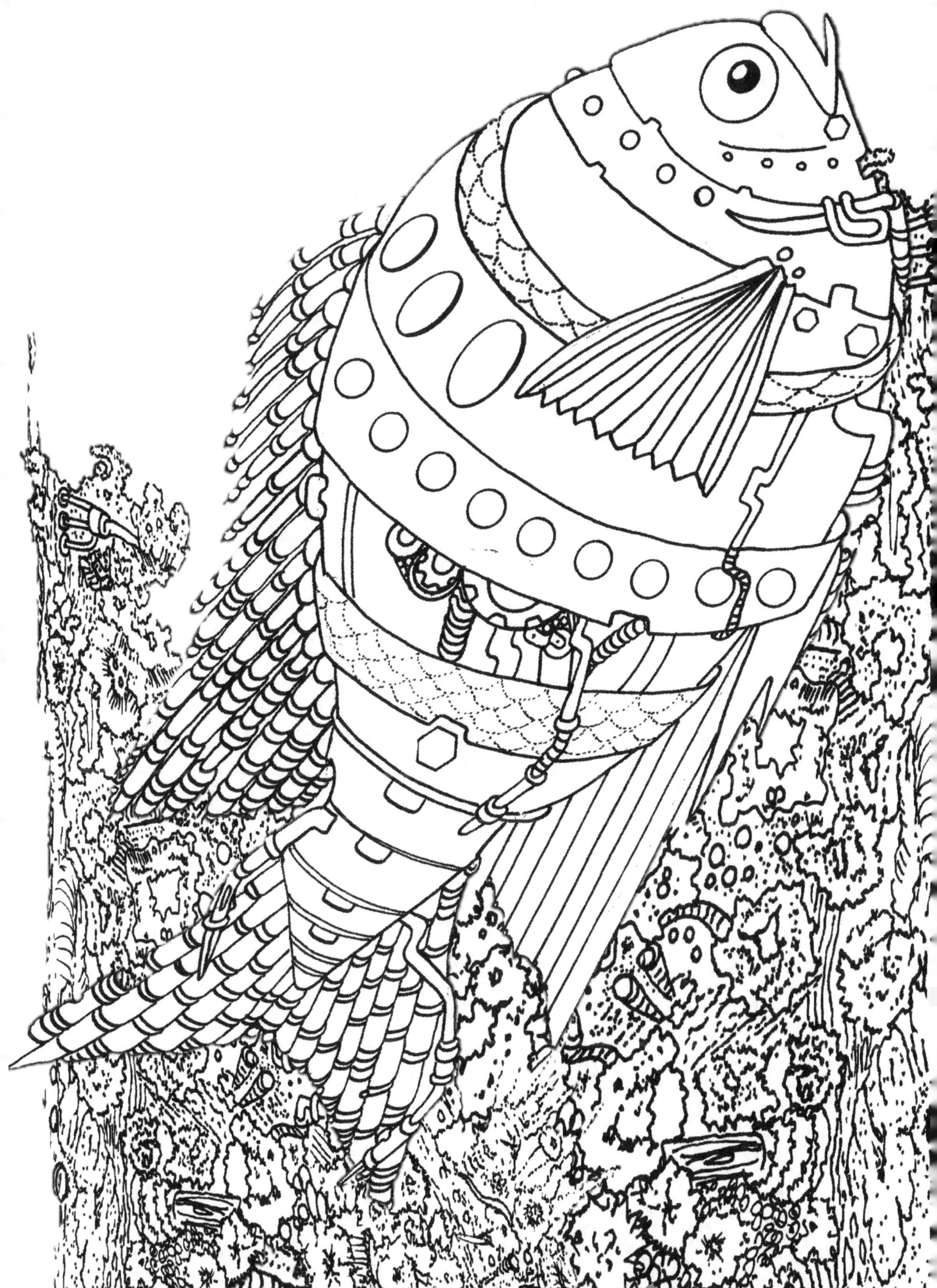

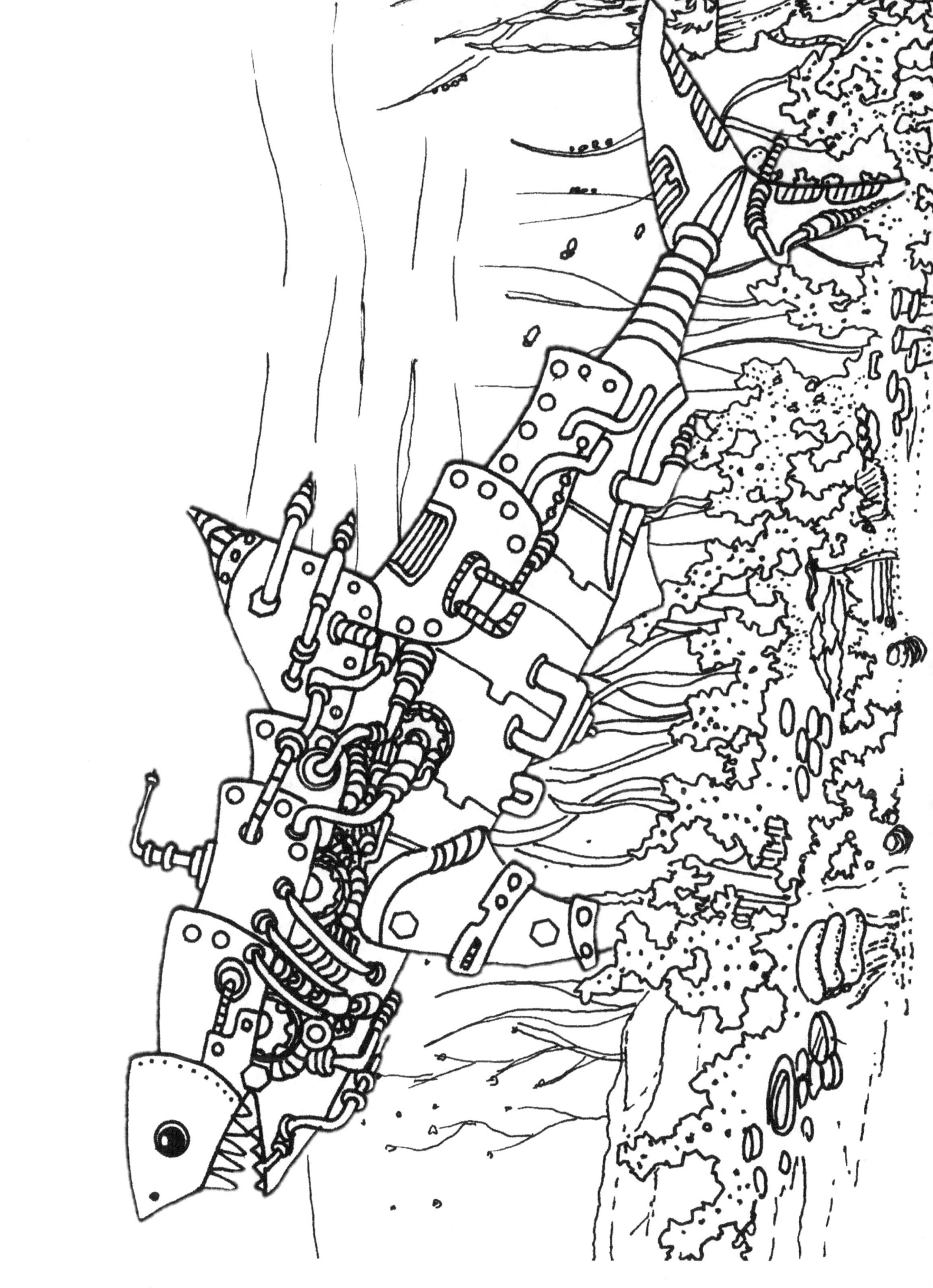

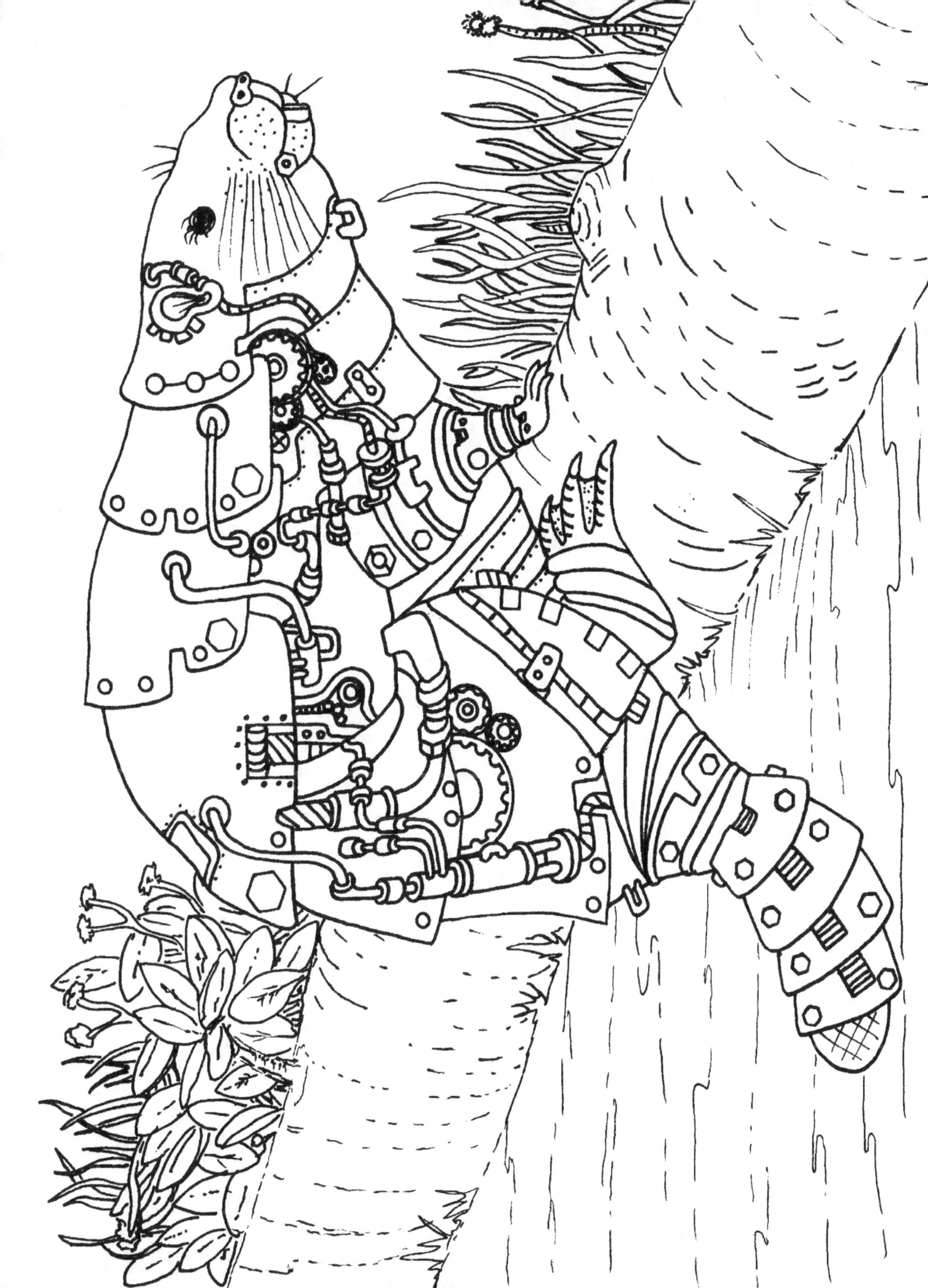

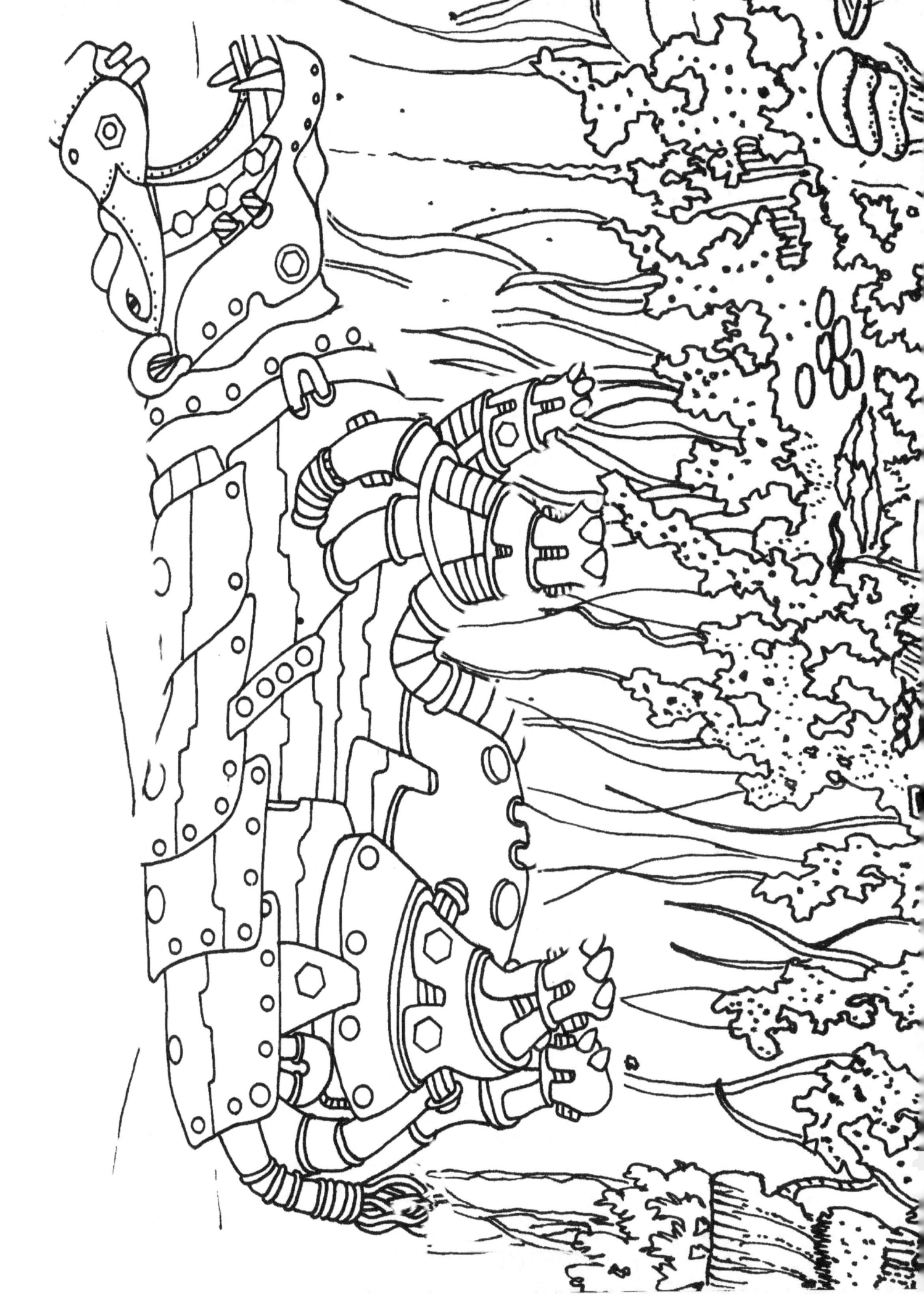

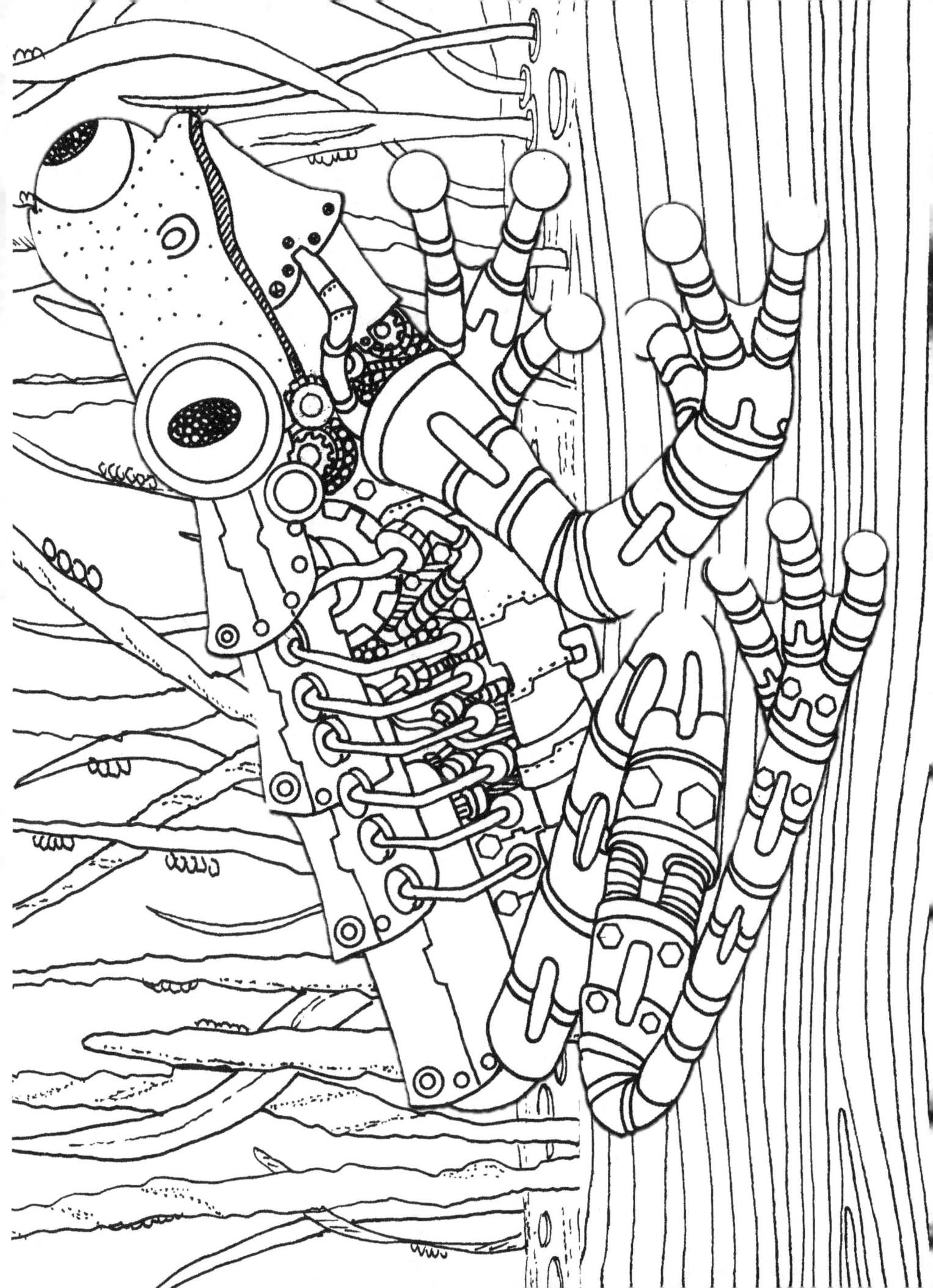

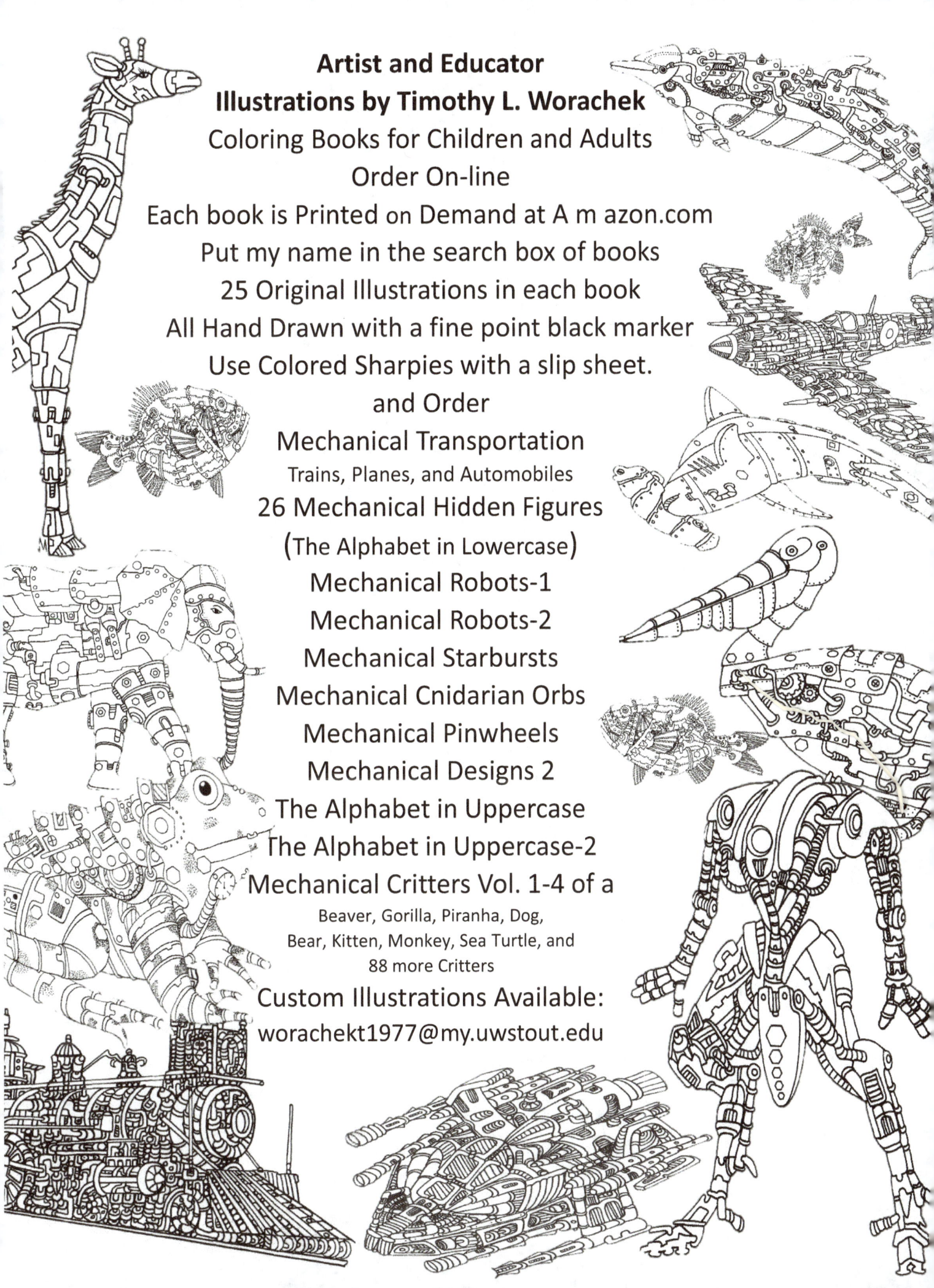

Artist and Educator
Illustrations by Timothy L. Worachek
Coloring Books for Children and Adults
Order On-line
Each book is Printed on Demand at A m azon.com
Put my name in the search box of books
25 Original Illustrations in each book
All Hand Drawn with a fine point black marker
Use Colored Sharpies with a slip sheet.
and Order
Mechanical Transportation
Trains, Planes, and Automobiles
26 Mechanical Hidden Figures
(The Alphabet in Lowercase)
Mechanical Robots-1
Mechanical Robots-2
Mechanical Starbursts
Mechanical Cnidarian Orbs
Mechanical Pinwheels
Mechanical Designs 2
The Alphabet in Uppercase
The Alphabet in Uppercase-2
Mechanical Critters Vol. 1-4 of a
Beaver, Gorilla, Piranha, Dog,
Bear, Kitten, Monkey, Sea Turtle, and
88 more Critters
Custom Illustrations Available:
worachekt1977@my.uwstout.edu